HOTEL HOBBIES

50 THINGS
TO DO IN A **HOTEL**
ROOM THAT WON'T
GET YOU ARRESTED

Marcus Weeks

HOTEL HOBBIES

THUNDER BAY
P · R · E · S · S

San Diego, California

THUNDER BAY PRESS
An imprint of the Advantage Publishers Group
5880 Oberlin Drive, San Diego, CA 92121-4794
www.thunderbaybooks.com

All notations of errors or omissions should be addressed to Thunder Bay Press, Editorial Department, at the above address. All other correspondence (author inquiries, permissions) concerning the content of this book should be addressed to The Ivy Press.

ISBN-13: 978-1-59223-532-2
ISBN-10: 1-59223-532-8
Library of Congress Cataloging-in-Publication Data available upon request.

Printed in Singapore
1 2 3 4 5 10 09 08 07 06

This book was conceived, designed, and produced by
THE IVY PRESS LIMITED
The Old Candlemakers, West Street,
Lewes, East Sussex BN7 2NZ, U.K.

Creative Director: Peter Bridgewater
Publisher: Sophie Collins
Editorial Director: Jason Hook
Art Director: Karl Shanahan
Designer: Simon Goggin
Illustrator: John Woodcock
Photography: Simon Punter
Hotel Hobbyists: Joanna Clinch/Anna Davies

ACKNOWLEDGMENTS
The publishers would like to thank the following for permission to reproduce their pictures:
© Karen Beard/Stone/
Getty Images (cover);
© Sean Justice/The Image Bank/Getty Images (title page).

Contents

Introduction

Hotels, for most people, offer the sort of glamour
and excitement normally associated with vacations
and honeymoons, a romantic rendezvous, or a
night on the town. For many, however, the glitz
has become dulled through overexposure—the
traveling salespeople, conference delegates,
and touring musicians, for example, who find
themselves in soulless hotel rooms more often
than their own comfortable bedrooms and alone
(or worse, with tedious colleagues) more often
than in the bosom of their families. It is to them
that this book is affectionately dedicated, and
for the improvement of their lot that it was
originally conceived.

People who have to stay in hotels for their work
will tell you that the tales of wild, all-night parties
and gratuitous sexual liaisons are exaggerated,

to say the least. The majority of hotel guests are more likely to be kept awake by bedroom boredom than by shameless shenanigans and will resort to all manner of pointless activities to relieve the mind-numbing monotony. But surely there's more to life than adult-TV channel-hopping, calling 1-900 numbers, picking the logo off the bathrobe, or confusing room service by placing orders that have bizarre dietary requirements—there must be a more creative use of the jaded inmate's downtime . . .

Well, of course there is! And here at last is a guide to the indoor crafts, games, and sports available to the hotel hobbyist—needing no extra equipment beyond the courtesy items found in hotel rooms and the contents of your carry-on luggage. With a little imagination and application, these projects could transform you from a sad, lonely couch potato into the kind of guy or gal who just can't find enough hours in the day. A note of caution, however—as with all hobbies, it may take some practice to acquire the necessary expertise. Don't be disappointed if your first attempts turn out less than stunning—although we've done our best to ensure you'll achieve something to be proud of, we can't guarantee success every time.

The more strenuous activities are not entirely without risk to personal safety, especially for those whose previous hotel lifestyles consisted of passive pursuits like snacking and drinking. Be realistic about your abilities, especially if you are generally unused to physical activity. And if you must include swinging from the light fixtures, for example, first check that they will take your weight. We hope this guide will inspire you and that you'll soon be making up hobbies and pastimes of your own. If you do, please let us know, so we can include them in another book.

WARNING

While the majority of these projects can be attempted safely, this book is intended only as a humorous reference source. No responsibility can be taken by the publishers or author for any loss, injury, or damage occasioned by reliance on the information contained herein. Care should always be taken to ensure that no damage is done to hotel property, and hobbies requiring physical exertion should not be attempted by anyone with health problems. If in doubt, seek professional advice.

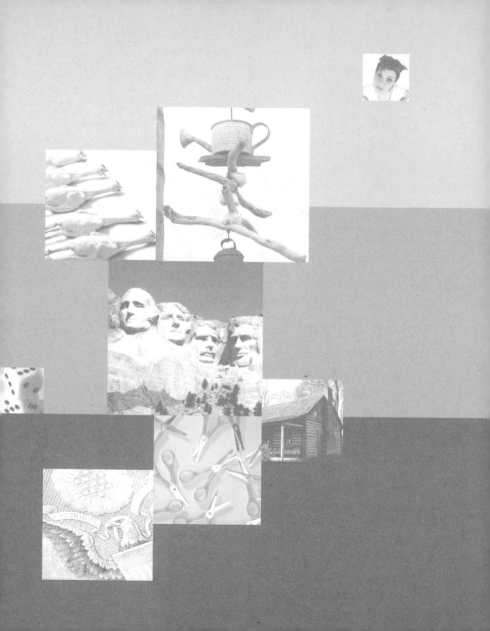

ARTS & CRAFTS

There's a long tradition of creative hobbying among those who find themselves away from home. It's possible that the first examples of art—cave paintings—are the work of Stone Age men killing time on long hunting trips. The timeless joy of a creative pastime is that it has an end product; not only do you get to fill your time usefully and acquire new skills, but you have something to show for it, too. This can take the shape of an ornament or trinket to brighten up your impersonal hotel room, or a gift you can take home for your loved ones. The joy they'll get in receiving the fruit of your labors can only be matched by the pride you'll feel in your newfound talents.

These days, you can show off your creations to a wider audience instantly via your cell phone—just take a photograph and send it to your friends and family. And although you might feel restricted at first by the limited materials available in your hotel room, with a little patience and imagination you'll soon discover a whole new world of creative possibilities.

Towel Origami

It is not written that origami should only be paper-based. Well, actually it is, because the word *origami* means "paper-folding" in Japanese, but things often get lost in translation. You will be amazed by the verisimilitude of this chicken (oven-ready rather than free-range), and the monkey with chocolate eyes will take the hotel hobbyist to new levels of origami originality.

Tip| *Like everything worthwhile, towel origami takes time to perfect. Do not waver from the Way of the Chicken. When you reach perfection, you will want to do it at home to impress friends and relatives. Turn your back while performing step 4— this way, the chicken will be a real surprise.*

YOU WILL NEED

Chicken
- HAND TOWEL

Monkey
- HAND TOWEL
  AND WASHCLOTH
  OR
  BATH TOWEL
  AND HAND TOWEL

- SUGAR GLUE
  (*see page 17*)

- COMPLIMENTARY
  CHOCOLATES

1| CHICKEN Lay the towel out with one of the short ends facing you. Smooth out any wrinkles. Take one end, pinch over each corner, pull taut, and roll to the center. Repeat with the other end.

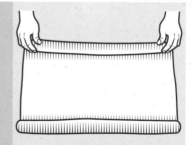

2| Hold the rolls firmly pressed down on the surface. Find the towel corner in the center of one end of one of the rolls and tug sharply, so that it pulls out like a telescope. Repeat for all four "points."

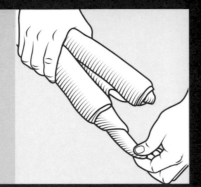

3| Pick up the towel by the four points, keeping those from each end together. Bring your hands together, and the towel will fold in half.

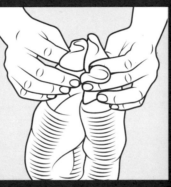

4| Carefully swap over one point from each hand to the other, so you are holding a point from each end of the towel in either hand. Hold the towel out and pull one set of feet downward: instant chicken.

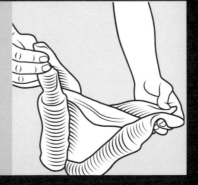

Continued on page 16

Towel Origami

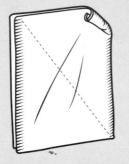

5| MONKEY To convert your chicken into a monkey, you need a head! Fold a towel in half. Roll the top right and bottom left corners diagonally into the center.

6| You now have a long, narrow shape. Roll the bottom point up to the top point. This will form a tight ball that is the basis for your monkey's head.

Tip| *You need to keep the monkey's head and body in proportion. For a large monkey, use a bath towel for the body and a hand towel for the head. For a smaller primate, try a hand towel for the body and a washcloth for the head.*

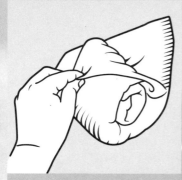

7| Turn the rolled shape over. Peel the top layer of the point back to cover the shape and form the mouth. Tuck all ends into the folds.

8| Use sugar glue to fix your monkey's head to his body. Add complimentary chocolates secured with sugar glue to create your monkey's eyes.

Tip| **SUGAR GLUE** *is the hotel hobbyist's adhesive of choice, using a cunning formula that combines sugar (found in packets in most hotel rooms) and water (found in all but the most basic hotels) to create a strong glue. Mix two parts sugar with one part hot water to form a thick syrup that hardens as it cools.*

Soap Scrimshaw

A manly activity for the hotel-bound, inspired by Captain Ahab and his merry whalers who used to spend downtime on the *Pequod* whittling presents out of whale teeth for the girls they left behind. Why not revive this art using those miniature soaps too small to wash with and your nail file or some minibar toothpicks? Think of famous figures or household objects. Start simple—a model of a cell phone, say—and keep at it until you can produce convincing family likenesses or a very small Mount Rushmore.

YOU WILL NEED

- BAR OF SOAP
- SHOWER CAP *(possibly)*
- NAIL FILE

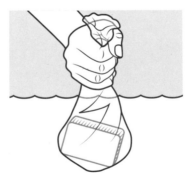

1| Soap that is too hard to be workable should be placed in a shower cap and briefly submerged in hot water.

Warning| *Do not let your finished work get wet, as it will melt and decompose. Take the land artist (e.g., Andy Goldworthy, Christo) option and photograph your work as soon as it's finished. E-mail pics to your family, so they know what you made for them (the soap may collapse in your toiletry bag on the way home).*

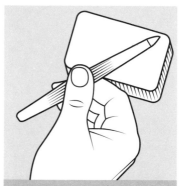

2| The nail file has two ends: a sharp point and a flat scoop. Use both ends for the best results.

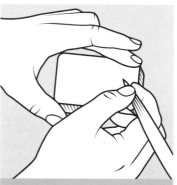

3| Try sculpting with the bar flat, making a relief picture with integrated frame.

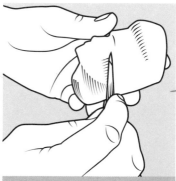

4| Angle the rasp section of the file when smoothing out lumpy or rough areas.

Shown here|
Inspiring examples of soap scrimshaw made earlier by advanced students— the Eiffel Tower, a generic cell phone, and a cameo Elvis.

Coat Hanger Wind Chimes

Here's a way to personalize your surroundings while at the same time minimizing bad vibes in your room. These decorative wind chimes not only look good as they glint in the light from the bedside lamp and provide a restful tinkling sound as they sway gently in the air-conditioning draft, they can also help to energize chi when strategically placed in auspicious positions (*see Sugar Zen Garden, page 54*). If the weather's good, you can hang one on the balcony to catch the breeze and drive away intrusive evil spirits.

Tip| *You need those thin wire coat hangers you get in cheap hotels. If there are only wooden or plastic ones, dangle small objects from them on threads; if they're integral to the wardrobe, work in situ to make a haven of positive karma to hang your power suit in.*

YOU WILL NEED

- WIRE COAT HANGERS
- DENTAL FLOSS OR THREAD FROM EMERGENCY SEWING KIT
- KEY OR TEASPOON
- PIECE OF PAPER

1| Take a wire coat hanger and bend the long side (opposite the hook) around into a circle. Tie the two angled sides together with dental floss or thread from a sewing kit. Bend them up until the hook is above the center of the circle.

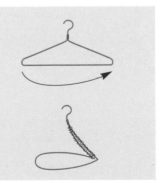

2| Unwind a second coat hanger below the hook. Straighten the two sides. Bend the angles back and forth until they break, giving you three lengths of wire. Break each into two unequal parts by bending back and forth.

3| Form a small hook at the end of each length of wire. You now have six chimes, which can be hung around the circumference of the frame using thread or dental floss.

4| Suspend a teaspoon or key within the circle of the frame to form a clapper that will strike all the chimes. Continue this thread below the clapper and attach a piece of paper to catch any drafts and activate the chimes.

Toothpick Pioneering

You're a long way from home, and probably a long way from the countryside too, but there's no reason not to indulge your inner frontiersperson. Why not build an authentic (but tiny) log cabin, somewhere your pocket Crockett can really get away from it all? Check out your checkered shirt and don your dungarees, then get down to some manly construction work on your own little home on the range. And when you have to leave that neck of the woods, you can take it with you for the little lady back home.

YOU WILL NEED

- DRINK COASTER
- TOOTHPICKS *(lots)*
- NAIL CLIPPERS
- SUGAR GLUE
  (see page 17)
- NAIL FILE
- DENTAL FLOSS
  OR THREAD
- HAIR SPRAY

Tip| *Half the fun of this project is getting hold of enough toothpicks for the job. You'll have to forage first, and this adds to the feeling of backwoodsmanship. There's bound to be a few in your room, but extra supplies will have to be garnered by forays to the hotel bar for raids on the olive and lemon bowls and carefully worded orders from room service.*

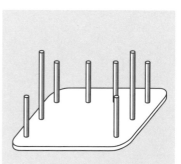

1| Make holes for upright beams in the coaster foundation. Cut toothpicks to size with nail clippers. Use sugar glue to stick the beams into the holes. Leave to set.

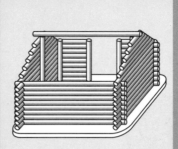

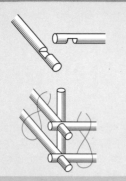

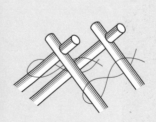

2| Using the nail file, file grooves into wall logs where they overlap at corners. Assemble around the upright beams; tie with dental floss to build up the walls.

3| For the top half of the wall, decrease the size of the logs to create the roof angle. Lay a ridge pole on which to put the roof.

4| Cut out windows where appropriate and glue in window frames using sugar glue. Make a door and hang it, using dental floss as hinges.

5| Lay roof poles over the ridge, tying them securely together. Give it all a coat of hair spray as a timber preservative. You now have a home where the buffalo roam.

Wine Cork Stamps

Remember those potato stamps you made as a kid in elementary school? How you could put your personal stamp on every surface in the house? Well, this is a grown-up version of the same thing, and what's more, it provides an excuse for drinking a bottle of wine by yourself without feeling guilty. Design your own logo for a seal to create personalized stationery, or cut hearts, flowers, or psychedelic patterns to decorate lamp shades, mirrors, furniture, clothing, luggage—the sky's the limit.

YOU WILL NEED

- WINE CORKS
- NAIL FILE, PENKNIFE, OR HOTEL CUTLERY
- JAM, COFFEE, TEA, RED WINE, OR SHOE POLISH
- TOOTHPICKS

Warning| *Lately, wine producers have been replacing traditional cork stoppers with plastic ones. This needn't stop you from using them— just make sure you cut off the end to expose the porous part in the middle of the stopper. If you have screw-top wine bottles, you've got more of a problem. Just enjoy the wine and try another project.*

1| Open the wine bottle. Take a slug while the cork dries. Cut a design into each end of the cork.

2 Experiment with designs. It helps to sketch them on paper first. Remember that everything will come out back-to-front when you start printing.

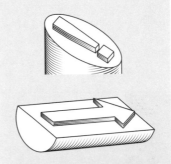

3 You can get larger and differently shaped stamps by cutting the cork lengthwise or obliquely before engraving your design.

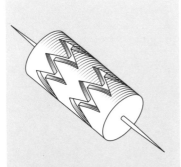

4 Continuous patterns can be made using the cork as a roller stamp with abstract designs; toothpicks pushed into the ends make nifty handles.

Tip *Put your chosen "ink" (red wine, very strong coffee or tea, or jam, for example) into a saucer, or use shoe polish straight from the can. Dunk the stamp in it. Test the result on a paper napkin. If you're happy with the result, start printing!*

Dental Floss Pom-poms

- GLASS
- DRINK COASTERS
- DENTAL FLOSS
- FINGERNAIL SCISSORS OR PENKNIFE

So, you've just watched the big game on TV, and your mind keeps straying back to your good old college days when you lusted after (or wanted to be) one of the cheerleaders. But what was it that made them so attractive? The fabulous figures? The sexy outfits? No, it was the pom-poms. Bring back the thrill of those heady days and inject a little rah-rah into your dull hotel room by making some for yourself or for the dental hygienist/cheerleader in your life.

Tip| *Use colored threads from your emergency sewing kit or picked off some unimportant clothing. Wind these threads in among the floss during step 2. Also consider dyeing floss with red wine, green mouthwash, or other toiletries.*

1| Using a glass as a guide, cut coasters into two disks of two or three inches in diameter. Cut one-inch circular holes in the middle. Don't worry if they're a bit eccentric— small inaccuracies won't ruin the end result.

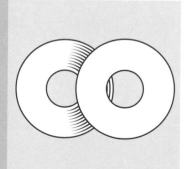

2| Put the disks together and wind a long piece of dental floss around and around them. Use extra lengths of floss as necessary, until the hole in the middle is closed up and the whole thing is fat and round.

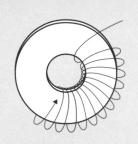

3| Insert a knife blade or scissors through the floss and between the two disks, then cut around the circumference.

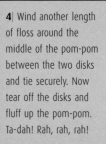

4| Wind another length of floss around the middle of the pom-pom between the two disks and tie securely. Now tear off the disks and fluff up the pom-pom. Ta-dah! Rah, rah, rah!

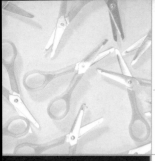

Do-Not-Disturb Decoupage

- "DO NOT DISTURB" SIGNS
- DRINK COASTERS
- PICTURE POSTCARDS
- LEAFLETS, HOTEL STATIONERY, MAGAZINES FROM LOBBY, ETC.
- FINGERNAIL SCISSORS
- SUGAR GLUE *(see page 17)*, JAM, OR HONEY

Do not disturb? No such luck. When you're bored to tears in your hotel room, you'd relish any interruption just to relieve the tedium. So just what can you use that "Do Not Disturb" sign for? How about reviving the Victorian craft of decoupage, cutting it into interesting shapes and sticking them, along with fragments of coasters, postcards, and flyers, in decorative patterns on lamp shades or on postcards to send home? You'll get so engrossed once you start that you really won't want to be disturbed.

Some suggestions to get you going . . .

It's simple, really—just cut out pictures, words, shapes, or anything that strikes you and stick them onto the surface you want to decorate. Use a strong sugar-and-water solution as your adhesive, or utilize the sticky qualities of that delicious complimentary jam.

MUG MASTERPIECE

Transform your coffee mug into an ornamental vase. Picture postcards or glossy magazine covers can provide suitable images for turning that mug into a masterpiece.

HANDMADE CARDS

Create handmade greeting cards. These cost a fortune in the gift shop but can be easily made, using the hotel stationery as a base, for a fraction of the price. Choose images and text fragments to suit the occasion.

PLAYING IT SAFE

Make an original artwork out of the room-service menu or telephone instructions. Use this as a base for letting your imagination soar. In more expensive hotels, these notices are often framed, which will make the finished picture look even more impressive.

LIVELY LAMP SHADE

Liven up a lamp shade. Decorate that uninspired bedside shade with a pattern of stripes and dots, or be daring and create an avant-garde random collage.

Tip| *You'll find this works best with stuff printed on cardboard or stiff paper, since it's easier to work with, gives an attractive relief texture, and the adhesive doesn't bleed through like it does with ordinary paper. Don't worry too much if you can't cut around shapes very accurately with your fingernail scissors—it kind of adds to the charm of the thing.*

Cut-Ups

If you're a fan of William Burroughs or John Cage, you'll love this sort of artless art. The basic philosophy is to create something unintentionally: you just do the drudgery, and luck will provide the aesthetic content. Taking mundane sources such as local guides, in-house magazines, and yesterday's newspaper, you can deconstruct the texts and imbue them with new meaning by reassembling them randomly on the page. Depending on your point of view, the result could be great literature, inspired nonsense, or total garbage, but with a bit of luck you'll find some kind of bizarre logic in there somewhere.

Warning| *The creator of this form of literature was notoriously inspired by his use of illicit substances, a practice we cannot condone. Neither can we recommend hitting the minibar to achieve that truly haphazard result, as you may wake up not only hungover but with random words and phrases stuck on various parts of your body, the bed, etc.*

YOU WILL NEED

- LOCAL GUIDES, LEAFLETS
- NEWSPAPERS AND MAGAZINES FROM THE LOBBY
- HOTEL STATIONERY
- FINGERNAIL SCISSORS
- SUGAR GLUE *(see page 17)* OR JAM OR HONEY

DEAD FINGERS TALK

Collect together as many different pieces of text as you can lay your hands on, and lay out a few sheets of hotel stationery as your base. Sit quietly and try to clear your mind of all rational thoughts.

NAKED TEAPOT

Cut random words and phrases from your texts and store them in a clean, dry coffee- or teapot. Give this a thorough shake, and pull out cuttings one by one, sticking them neatly onto the paper in the order they come— don't be tempted to read them at this stage! Continue until you've run out of words, paper, or patience. Now try reading the result. Weird, huh?

2

EDIBLE PLEASURES

Yes, I know there's a perfectly reasonable restaurant and bar downstairs, but you can't spend all evening down there, can you? How sad would that be? Besides, the hotel has kindly provided the culinary ingredients for a full evening's entertainment right there in your room.

First, there's the minibar. For some professional guests, this is just a means of achieving oblivion, but for the hotel hobbyist it's a treasure trove. It's not just the contents of the bottles, though of course they have all sorts of creative possibilities, but the little bottles themselves—there's almost no end to the games you can devise with them. Then there's the breakfast tray, with a hobbyist's palette ranging from honey to coffee. And don't forget the dishes and cutlery—very useful for the hotel handyperson. Finally, you've got the little bars of chocolate, the cookies, and the complimentary fruit bowl. Who could wish for a better-equipped little studio? There's just no excuse for frittering away your time in the bar with everyone else when you've got so much to keep you busy right there in your room.

Minibar Cocktails

See how many different, very tiny cocktails you can make using only the contents of the minibar. Make a Manhattan first (*see recipe, opposite*) to get the juices flowing, then make as many off-the-wall drinks as you can think of. Try and remember to write down the recipe each time (before you drink it), then grade it on a scale of one to ten. Put the list somewhere safe. That way, when you play this game again, you will not duplicate your hangover. Whoever makes the widest variety of cocktails out of one minibar is the winner. You won't remember that you're playing solo.

Some suggestions to get you going . . .

You could certainly attain a Screwdriver, and although there's usually only one kind of rum and no brandy in your average minibar, you could attempt a sort of half-Zombie—more of a Heavy Sleeper, really. But it's more fun to make it up as you go along. Don't forget to think outside the minibar, and be fearless about adding new and unusual ingredients to the mix. These will get more innovative and exciting as the evening wears on, but you may not notice.

Here is a selection of delicious cocktails. See if you can guess which ones we made up.

MANHATTAN
1½ oz. whiskey or bourbon, ¾ oz. sweet vermouth, dash of bitters (if available)

Build in a rocks glass, or stir over ice and strain into a chilled cocktail glass. Garnish with a cherry.

NEXT TIME, I'LL EAT THE CHOCOLATE
Your complimentary chocolate (left on pillow by bed-making operatives) cut up small (use your nail file), 2 oz. Baileys, 1 oz. rum, ice

Put the chocolate shards in a long glass with the Baileys. Cover with a coaster and shake hard. In another glass, pour rum over crushed ice, then slowly add Baileys mixture. Stir.

BRITISH ICED TEA
Ice, tea bag, any alcohol you have left, club soda

Put ice in glass, drape tea bag over it. Add alcohol and club soda. Leave to infuse for 40 minutes, or until dark brown. Remove tea bag (save for eye pad in the morning). Sip.

SCREWDRIVER
1¼ oz. vodka, orange juice

Serve over ice in highball glass or coffee mug.

MINT DESPERADO
Spoonful or cube of sugar, 2 oz. whiskey, squeeze of toothpaste

Put sugar in glass, add whiskey. Squeeze in toothpaste to taste. Stir slightly. Drink. This is good as a nightcap: it automatically cleans your teeth for you.

ADHD
Energy drink, red wine, cola, half-glass of sugar

Shake ingredients together and drink in one slurp. Now try En Suite Free Running (*see page 74*).

ZOMBIE
2 oz. light rum, 1 oz. dark rum, 1 oz. apricot brandy, splash simple syrup, pineapple juice, and 151% rum

Blend first two rums, brandy, simple syrup, and pineapple juice with ice. Pour into collins or hurricane glass. Float the 151% rum on top.

continued on page 38

MOCK MOCHA

Complimentary chocolate, instant coffee, sugar, hot water, large shot of rum or brandy

Create chocolate shavings by scraping with nail file or penknife and mix these with an individual package of instant coffee and sugar to taste. Add just enough hot water to dissolve these ingredients and form a thin syrup. Leave to cool, then add spirits and stir.

CHUCK'S FIZZ

Freshly squeezed orange juice (from the fruit basket), white wine, effervescent hangover cure tablet

Squeeze the juice of a couple of oranges into a highball glass, then top up with white wine and chill. Pop in the effervescent tablet and drink while it's still fizzing for maximum effect. It may not taste too good, but you'll feel okay in the morning.

GIN SLING (POOR MAN'S PIMM'S)

Slices of fruit, cucumber, and watercress garnish from a room service sandwich, ice, a large slurp of gin, small cup of cold, strong black tea, club soda

Put the fruit and vegetables into an empty water pitcher with ice, then pour over the gin, tea, and club soda. Wonderful for those long, hot summer evenings.

PINK (OR BLUE OR GREEN) GIN
Dash of Angostura bitters (or, if unavailable, a few drops of mouthwash), gin

Roll the bitters (or mouthwash) around the inside of a tumbler until it is evenly coated. Pour in a shot of gin and add ice to taste. Not for the fainthearted.

TEQUILA MOCKINGBIRD
Pinch of salt, wedge of lemon or lime, shot of vodka

(Who knows, you may find yourself in a Mexican hotel sometime where you could try the real thing, but until then you can make do with vodka—or after the first couple, just about anything). Place a pinch of salt on the soft part between your thumb and forefinger, and hold the fruit in your other hand. Take a good suck on the lime or lemon, then knock your wrist so that the salt jumps into your mouth. Okay, try again. Once you can do this in one fluid movement, reward yourself by knocking back the spirit in one gulp.

Tip *Get the authentic feel of a cocktail bar by presenting your drinks prettily. Try frosting the edge of the glass by wetting the rim and dipping it in sugar, and serving some of your cocktails over ice crushed in a plastic bag with the heel of your shoe. Decorating with slices of fruit helps too, as do stuffed olives acquired from downstairs. To add the finishing touch, try that useless plastic coffee stirrer as a swizzle stick, and make yourself a cocktail umbrella out of toothpicks and a paper napkin.*

Minibar Bottle Band

Don't you hate the music on local radio stations and the endless pop videos on cable TV? Not to mention the aural wallpaper incessantly seeping into the hotel lobby. There's nothing to beat a live performance, especially if you're the one calling the tune. With a little ingenuity, you can turn the contents of your minibar into a miniband and spend the evening jamming to the songs you like. The folks back home shouldn't miss out on your musical talents; just give them a call and play them your latest composition.

YOU WILL NEED

- BOTTLES FROM MINIBAR
- DRINKING STRAW *(preferably plastic bendable one)*
- WASTEBASKET
- METAL TRAY
- GLASSES, TEACUPS, COFFEE MUG, WATER PITCHER
- TEASPOON, TOOTHBRUSH
- DENTAL FLOSS *(for bass)*

Tip| *When you've achieved a scale you're happy with, mark the levels on the minibar bottles with a pen. You may want to inspire your composing skills with another drink at some stage, so you'll have to top off any empties with water.*

1| WIND SECTION Take eight bottles from the minibar. Drink enough to give a different note out of each when you blow across the top.

2| Arrange the bottles in a line on your dressing table, with the lowest-pitched sounding one on the left, going up to the highest pitch on the right.

3| If you want some sultry low notes, use the mouthwash, shower gel, or shampoo bottles from the bathroom, or a couple of large wine bottles.

4| Make a tiny oboe out of a drinking straw. Flatten one end and cut small holes at intervals along its length. Squeeze the flat end between your lips.

5| Blow extremely hard while covering and uncovering the holes. If you have flexible straws, you can convert your oboe to a sax for instant Charlie Parker.

continued on page 42

Minibar Bottle Band

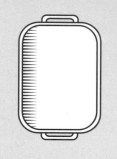

6| **THE PERCUSSION SECTION** Use an upturned wastebasket for your bass drum. You can play this by stamping on it with you right foot.

7| A suspended metal tray will make a good cymbal. Set up your kit to the right of the bottles on the dressing table.

Tip| *If you've got a pocket cassette recorder or some way of recording on your laptop, lay down a few tracks for posterity. You might want to write it down too, either in musical notation if you can, or in some kind of numerical notation of your own devising.*

8| Glasses, mugs, and bottles make great percussion instruments. Use teaspoons for sticks—or if you want that cool jazzy sound, try a shaving brush or toothbrush.

9| THE BASS Tie a length of dental floss to the corners of the dressing table. Pluck with your left hand and stretch with your foot for different notes.

10| Set up a funky groove with the bass (left hand and/or foot) and drums (right hand), then get on down and really express yourself with the horns.

Warning| *Not all guests share your appreciation of fine music, and some may even object to your practice sessions. There's no accounting for taste. Just so there are no nasty incidents, show a little consideration for these philistines by closing the show around midnight.*

Minibar Chess

YOU WILL NEED

- PAPER NAPKINS

- FELT-TIP PEN

- BOTTLES FROM MINIBAR
  (use caps for pawns)

- SCRAPS OF PAPER

- TOOTHPICKS

The main problem with mind-numbing boredom is just that—if you're not careful, your brain degenerates into a vegetative state in a matter of minutes—so it's vital to keep the little gray cells ticking away. There's no better form of intellectual gymnastics than a hard-fought battle on the chessboard—but how much more satisfying it is to play the game of kings with a set you've made yourself. OK, unless you can find a congenial colleague, you're going to have to play yourself, but some consolation is the rule that every time either of you take a piece, you have to drink it.

Warning| *The more successful you are in wiping your opponent off the board, the more liquor you will have consumed. This can lead to reckless moves that leave you wide open to attack, forcing a disappointing endgame. But since you're playing yourself, who cares?*

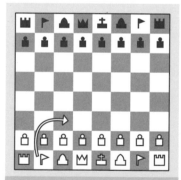

1| Join four napkins together and mark the eight-by-eight chessboard with a felt-tip pen. This board can be reused for Olive Pit Checkers (*see page 102*).

2| To distinguish between black and white, use clear bottles contrasted with brown and green, or simply play gin versus whiskey, for example. If it's a problem finding all 32 pieces, you can easily manage with 16 by using the caps as pawns.

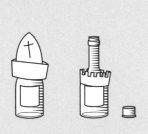

3| Stick on scraps of paper and toothpicks to create the distinguishing marks for each piece—a cross for the king, crown for the queen, miter for the bishop, pennant and shield for the knight, crenellations for the rook.

4| Grand Masters Smirnoff (white) and Johnny Walker (black) do battle. This is the first time they have faced each other across (or under) the table. Expect a spirited match, Smirnoff moving like a well-oiled machine and Walker playing a very tight game.

Jam Painting

- PLATE
  (or paper, or cookie)

- JAM, MARMALADE,
  HONEY, PEANUT BUTTER

- NAIL FILE, CUTLERY,
  TOOTHBRUSH, TOOTHPICK

- COASTER

Jam is a neglected medium, overlooked by all the major artists. Don't let this put you off—they probably laughed at the guy who suggested mixing eggs in to make tempera. It's not a good idea to attempt a mural, as it upsets the cleaning staff, so use a plate for your canvas. Apply the contents of the jars however you choose—smear it, daub it, build it up in impasto layers, or splatter it from your toothbrush. Because of the impermanence (and stickiness) of the materials, it's unlikely to end up hanging in the Guggenheim, but it will certainly brighten up your bedroom wall.

Tip| *Choose your subject carefully, bearing in mind your limited color range. Sunsets are good (plenty of reds and yellows), as are desert scenes (stripes of honey and peanut butter), but landscapes are tricky (you don't often get gooseberry jam in hotels), and seascapes are a definite no-no (even blueberry jam doesn't quite do it).*

1| Cool your materials in the fridge, then lay out a background by smearing on the first layer of jam with finger, nail file, or toothpick. Cool again.

Some suggestions . . .

You can use the jams straight from the jar or take some out and put it on a coaster palette—that way you can experiment with mixing colors. Get your creative juices flowing by attempting some different subjects. Here's a few to think about:

➲ Self-portrait

➲ View from the hotel window

➲ Still life with flowers and fruit

➲ Abstract

➲ Favorite painter's style in jam (Jam Gogh, Mondrijam, Jambrandt, Jam Ray . . .)

3| Harden in the fridge, *et voilà!* You have created your very own motel masterpiece.

2| Build up layers, thin out, wiping or licking away excess as necessary, and paint in details. Continue until you are pleased with the result.

Condiment collage

If you enjoyed the jam painting but would like to try something a bit more modern, or you prefer a more textural approach, try a collage using all the little packets of sauces and condiments you've collected on your travels. These provide an interesting surface to stick stuff onto—scraps of newspaper for a topical atmosphere capturing the Zeitgeist, bus tickets and hotel literature for local color, or pieces of the packets for formal coherence. Eat your heart out, Monsieur Matisse!

The Hotel Farm

Perhaps the most creative of all hobbies is gardening, and there's no reason not to indulge in a little hotel horticulture. Your seed catalog is right there in the fruit bowl and olive dish, and your plot is the breakfast tray filled with soil from the potted plants in the atrium. But why restrict yourself to a garden when you can create a whole farm—and even go into small-scale cheese and butter production! Unfortunately, you'll have to stick to land farming (unless it's a really bad hotel, where you could domesticate the rats).

1| FARM Spread soil (smuggled from plants in the lobby) over your breakfast tray. Smooth with a teaspoon. Divide into separate fields with toothpick picket fences and napkin hedges. Enrich the soil by using a fork to rake in ash from an ashtray in the hotel bar. Plow furrows with a nail file. Plant fruit and olive pits using a toothpick dibble, and rake over with a fork. Take sprout cuttings from egg sandwiches and plant in rows.

YOU WILL NEED

- SOIL FROM PLANTS, ASH FROM ASHTRAY

- BREAKFAST TRAY

- TEASPOON, FORK

- TOOTHPICKS, NAPKINS

- NAIL FILE

- FRUIT AND OLIVE PITS, SPROUT CUTTINGS

- DRINKING STRAWS

- DENTAL FLOSS

- INDIVIDUAL CREAMERS

- WIRE COAT HANGER

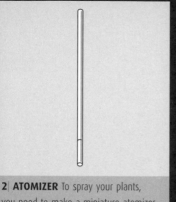

2| ATOMIZER To spray your plants, you need to make a miniature atomizer. Cut almost through a straw two inches from the end.

3| Place the straw in a glass of water, and bend the end to a 90-degree angle. Blow through the straw to create a miniature crop spray.

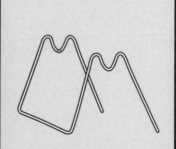

4| CHURN To create a butter churn, use dental floss to strap two sealed creamer containers to a drinking straw. Bend the end of the straw into a crank.

5| Bend a metal coat hanger into a frame. Rest the straw on it. Turn, turn, turn the crank until the milk, the cream, or your brain eventually turns to butter.

3

RITUALS & CEREMONIES

Let's face it, hotels are not the most spiritual places. As well as being soul-destroyingly impersonal, most have about as much aura as the average IRS office. After a few nights in these sterile surroundings, you're going to end up losing touch with your inner self (or maybe just losing your marbles), unless you do something about it. Luckily, there's a lot you can do to change your environment—and even yourself—for the better, by tapping into the ancient wisdom of cultures a world away from that bleak room.

And that's not all. Quite apart from making your hotel room a more restful and welcoming place, you will be able to make some positive steps toward improving all aspects of your life—your chances of success in business and romance, fame and fortune, and health and wealth are all increased by practicing these age-old arts. And that's got to be better than just killing time, doesn't it? So give it a try—tune in to your spiritual side and discover that these rituals and ceremonies have the power to transform your humdrum hotel stay into a life-enhancing and very beautiful experience.

53

Sugar Zen Garden

Use sugar from the packets on your coffee tray. Spread it out in an ashtray or soap dish to make your zen garden and rake with a fork. Make different patterns every day for the length of your stay, going for especially auspicious patterns to prepare for that important meeting, get that raise, improve your love life, or finish that difficult third album. Place the finished garden in the appropriate corner of the room for the intended enterprise (*see column on left*), and make sure it has an uninterrupted, energizing light source.

1| YIN/YANG GARDEN The yin/yang symbol is a great centering image for the jet-lagged and dislocated.

ADVANCED WORK 1:
If possible, use brown and white sugar to get a nice, balancing yin/yang thing going.

ADVANCED WORK 2:
Wet some of the sugar so it clumps into rocks. In the Zen tradition, rocks are used to signify treasure islands.

2| RAISE/PROMOTION Rake white sugar into auspicious waves. Rake brown sugar into $, £, or €, to taste.

3| A SUCCESSFUL LOVE LIFE Trace this sensual line across your garden to raise tantric energy levels.

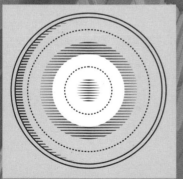

4| CLINCH A DEAL Make concentric circles, focusing cosmic attention on the central "treasure" rock.

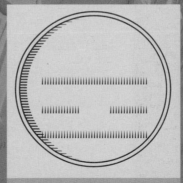

5| FAME Trace two parallel lines with a broken one in between to form li, the fame trigram.

Instant Mehndi (for women)

- VERY STRONG COFFEE
- MAKEUP BRUSH
- TOOTHPICK

Mehndi is the Indian art of painting decorative and auspicious patterns on your hands and feet, allowing you to unleash your creativity and wear your heart on your sleeve (or rather, just below it). Traditionally, this is done with henna. Now that's something you don't often find in hotels, but a similar effect can be achieved using coffee. This has the advantage of being less permanent than henna, so if you don't like your design, you can change it easily—and you can wash it off before that important sales meeting.

Some suggestions to get you going . . .

Although coffee is not a permanent marker, you'll probably feel happier planning your designs on paper before committing to skin. Try simple patterns until you get the hang of it, then move on to more complex ones incorporating signs and symbols with some great personal significance. Make a small cup of very strong coffee (black, no sugar please). Put on some sitar music and light a couple of incense sticks while you allow the coffee to cool.

1| Use your lip brush or a toothpick to paint the coffee onto your hands in auspicious patterns—swirling lines, triangles, hearts, flowers, and similar designs.

2| If you are not ambidextrous, you may have some problems painting the hand you favor; you might like to do your feet instead.

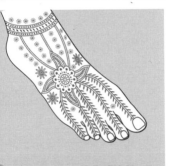

Tip| *Relax and admire your artwork while you allow yourself to dry. You are your own mehndi masterpiece!*

Instant Mehndi (for men)

The sort of macho equivalent of mehndi is the tattooing practiced by Maori males in New Zealand. After an enervating day at a conference, you may need to reassert your individuality and get in touch with your masculine side—what better way to do this than by using the resources of your hotel room to emulate the Maoris? Once you've painted on a design that expresses the inner you, you can devise a personal ritual dance to take out those frustrations and connect with earth spirits . . . and maybe take up rugby.

Some suggestions to get you going . . .

Your coffee tattoos are suitable not only for hands and feet, but for face and body also. To go the extra mile, you should simply strip to the waist and give yourself a broader canvas. Doing your back will not only have a dramatic effect, but will provide hours of fun. Use a toothpick and your fingers to paint your face in auspicious patterns. Try adding highlights with toothpaste and shoe polish. This is best done in front of the bathroom mirror, especially if you are not used to applying makeup.

YOU WILL NEED

- VERY STRONG COFFEE
- TOOTHPICK
- TOOTHPASTE
- SHOE POLISH

1| Use a toothpick to apply coffee in tattoo designs. Be creative—why not try incorporating your company logo to give yourself a tribal identity?

2| Allow your designs to dry before attempting to pull intimidating faces at the mirror in the Maori manner.

Tip| *Your transformation from coffee-drinking geek to tattooed warrior will only really be complete once you have attempted a traditional Maori welcoming dance.*

Hotel Numerology

Lots of hotels don't have a room number 13, some don't even have a 13th floor; most people have a lucky number, and some a number they avoid. But there's more to it than simple superstition. Numerology could provide the reason why you feel strongly about some numbers and even names, and you don't have to be an Einstein to find out more. Consult the chart to figure out what your room number signifies, or what the name of the hotel really means. Do they add up to peace and prosperity, or is it time to make some changes?

Tip| *Once you get going on this, you'll find there are all sorts of numbers and names you can work on. You may have problems, however, when staying in countries that do not use the Roman alphabet, or when you're not sure of the correct spelling of a name. Your problem, not mine.*

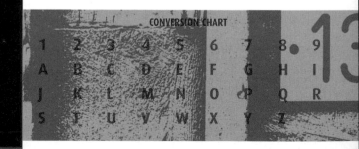

CONVERSION CHART

1	2	3	4	5	6	7	8	9
A	B	C	D	E	F	G	H	I
J	K	L	M	N	O	P	Q	R
S	T	U	V	W	X	Y	Z	

Here's how to figure out the spiritual significance of your name and number.

ROOM WITH AN INNER VIEW

• Add up the separate digits of the number of your room; if this comes to a two-digit number other than 11 or 22, add these together until you have 1, 2, 3, 4, 5, 6, 7, 8, 9, 11, or 22.

• Refer to the chart above to find the inner meaning of this number.

• Ponder this, and see how it applies to your situation. If you are unhappy with the reading, try changing to another room.

SPIRITUAL CELL

• Work out the numerological significance of your/your boss's/your loved one's cell phone number using the same method.

NAME NOT A NUMBER

• Using the conversion chart on page 58, convert your hotel name, your own name, or a business rival's name to numbers.

• For example, "Hotel" makes 8+6+2+5+3 = 24, 2+4 = 6. Use the chart above to figure out the numerological significance.

Feng Shui Your Room

YOU WILL NEED

- A GOOD SENSE OF DIRECTION

- NAIL SCISSORS

You know as soon as you walk into a room whether it feels right. And nine times out of ten, hotel rooms just don't. You can't do much about the position (overlooking the gas pipes) and color scheme (gray) without changing rooms or finding another hotel, but the principles of feng shui will help to make it more habitable. Once you've rearranged your furniture to maximize the positive energy flows and placed your knickknacks to harmonize with nature, you'll find it's a happier place to live and work in. With luck, improved health, well-being, and fortune will be yours, too.

Some suggestions to get you going . . .

Decide where to put your bed, furniture, and mirrors. It's best not to have the bed directly opposite the main entrance, facing away from it, or under a window; the head should be against something solid, with plenty of space at the foot and tall furniture to your left as you lie in it, lower furniture to your right. Do not put mirrors directly opposite doors or windows, because they reflect energy right back.

HOBBYIST'S FENG SHUI PLANNER

The grid on the right represents your room. It's divided into nine areas relating to your life. Always align it in relation to the wall with the entrance. Your goal is to place the most auspicious furniture and objects in each area you wish to influence, using the guide below. Use nail scissors to cut out the objects and placing them on the diagram. Then move your furniture around the room until it matches the diagram as closely as possible. It's a bit like a giant jigsaw puzzle. Keep in mind your desired outcome—do you want success in business, lustful good fortune, or just a good night's sleep?

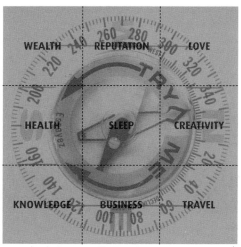

ENTRANCE

Place the cut-outs on the room grid to help your planning.

AUSPICIOUS ITEMS

WEALTH: Money, jewelry, fish, fountains, red, purple, gold

REPUTATION: Candles, awards, plants, red, orange, purple

LOVE: Round mirrors, pictures of loved ones, paired items, pink

HEALTH: Plants

SLEEP: Keep free for pacing up and down when you can't sleep

CREATIVITY: Paintings, hobby equipment

KNOWLEDGE: Books, manuals

BUSINESS: Mirrors, water, laptop

TRAVEL: Photos of helpers, colleagues

Create a Voodoo Shrine

The main purpose of voodoo rituals is to make contact with the spirits and obtain their help in your endeavors (improving your standard of living and good health, or dulling your business rival's edge, for instance). You could schlep off down to Haiti or New Orleans in order to communicate with the Loa (voodoo gods), but why not construct a voodoo temple in your room and perform your own ceremony? It's not difficult to get into a trancelike state after a day of meetings, although chanting and dancing might help.

YOU WILL NEED

- SHRINE-MAKING STUFF (candles, symbolic items, a central pole—a curtain pole, or a broom borrowed from the janitor's closet)

- WASTEBASKET AND RATTLE (empty can filled with sugar)

- SOAP

- PINS

Warning| *Don't mess with voodoo if your motives are less than pure. That old black magic's powerful stuff, and it could easily backfire if you don't know what you're doing. Calling on the spirit world has its drawbacks —zombies are really not at all pleasant and do have the tendency to severely disrupt your night's sleep . . . permanently.*

1| Clear a space around your dressing table. At its center, put up a pole as a *poteau-mitan*—this represents the axis of the world through which the Loa travel.

2| Decorate your dressing table with candles and objects symbolically linked to the Loa. It's customary to feast before voodoo ceremonies: go to the restaurant.

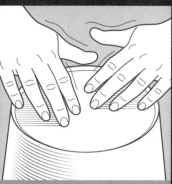

3| Start the ritual by beating a drum (wastebasket) and shaking a rattle (empty can half-filled with sugar).

Shown here| *Dance and chant to call the spirits down. If this doesn't work, try sacrificing the contents of the minibar. You will eventually fall into a trance and be possessed by the spirit of the Loa. You can also make a voodoo doll (not recommended, but it's expected in voodoo). Carve a likeness of the person or organization you wish to curse out of soap (see Soap Scrimshaw, page 16). They will be possessed by an obsessive need to wash.*

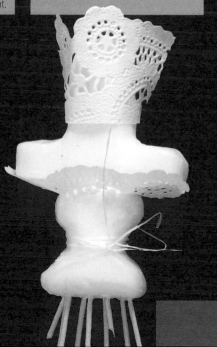

4

EXTREME SPORTS

Is your lifestyle too sedentary? Are you beginning to wonder if a little physical exercise might help tone up that bulging waistline? Do you find the hotel gym too boring (or intimidating, or just plain embarrassing)? Don't give up on the idea of a workout—you can get yourself into shape and enjoy the thrill of fast-moving sports right there in the privacy of your hotel room! And when you're done, you don't have to put up with other people's smelly gym shoes, sloppy hygiene, and macho horseplay, and you get to use your own changing room and shower.

Of course, you could just do a few push-ups or a little jogging in place without the need for any equipment at all, and such exercises might be useful as a warm-up. But it's far more satisfying to do some real circuit training or participate in a more challenging sport. So, unpack the tracksuit and sneakers, and prepare to blow away those cobwebs and get fit the hotel hobbyist way. Before you know it, you'll be laughing at the guys waiting for the elevator, even if your room's on the seventeenth floor.

69

Pants Press-Ups

Forget all that state-of-the-art gym equipment—treadmills, exercise bikes, and rowing machines—all you need for a satisfying workout is the pants presser lurking in the corner of the room. With this marvel of modern technology as your gym buddy, you can devise a fitness regime that will soon have your biceps bulging and create a six-pack the envy of the conference circuit. Just clear a space in the middle of the room and set up the presser as your workout center. Well, you're not going to use it for your clothes, are you?

Warning| *While every care has been taken in devising exercises for the pants presser, the publishers cannot accept responsibility for any mishaps or injury. Ensure presser is firmly set up, unplugged, and cool. If pants press is attached to the wall, hotel hobbyists are advised not to attempt steps 4 and 5.*

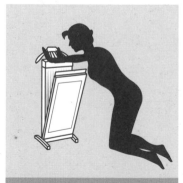

1| HALFWAY PRESS-UPS Hands on coat-hanger apparatus, body at 45-degree angle, push up. Advanced: feet on top of press and hands on bed (or even floor).

2| SQUATS Hold coat-hanger apparatus to steady yourself, and, er, squat. Give me twenty.

3| VAULT Use the pants presser as a vaulting horse. If you are going to attempt somersaults, use your mattress as a mat for soft landings.

4| WEIGHT LIFTING I Rest foot of press on the floor as standard. Now grip either side of coat-hanger apparatus and lift. Always keep a straight back.

5| WEIGHT LIFTING II With press set up on bed/chair as above, lie on your back with top of press resting on your chest. Now push top end up and down.

Toilet Tennis

YOU WILL NEED

- SPONGE
- LOOFAH OR LONG-HANDLED SCRUBBING BRUSH
- PLASTIC WRAP

Wonderful game, tennis. But difficult to play late at night, during the winter months, or when you're miles away from the nearest court, and even more difficult when you're alone and without your racket. Don't despair—you don't have to neglect your forehand or give up on your rallies: pop into the bathroom and you'll find everything you need for a set or two of practice. The loofah (or even better, a long-handled back-scrubbing brush) can be used as a racket, and the sponge makes an ideal ball; the toilet doubles as your court and opponent. Anyone for toilet tennis?

1| TENNIS Lift toilet lid and ensure plastic wrap is tightly stretched over toilet seat for maximum bounce.

Warning| *Before starting your practice session, remove all mats and obstacles from the playing area. Bathroom floors are notoriously slippery when wet, so take time to dry them thoroughly, and wear nonslip footwear, if possible. There's also a fair amount of glassware in bathrooms, so don't take the forehand smash too literally.*

2 Mark boundaries with soap or lipstick. Serve, aiming to bounce the sponge off the plastic wrap and back of toilet and back, so that you can practice your return.

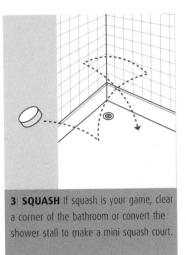

3 SQUASH If squash is your game, clear a corner of the bathroom or convert the shower stall to make a mini squash court.

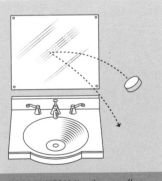

4 BADMINTON Use the cap off an aerosol can (deodorant or shaving cream, for instance) as a shuttlecock, and bounce it off the mirror above the sink.

En Suite Free Running

YOU WILL NEED

- ENERGY
- NERVES OF STEEL

A relative newcomer to the sports scene, free running is catching on in a big way. Although it's normally associated with the outdoor urban environment, there's no reason why you shouldn't adapt it to your hotel room. The goal is to see if you can get all the way around your room and the en suite area without touching the ground. The rules are simple, but it will take all your ingenuity and skill—jumping, bouncing, swinging, and clambering—to complete the course. If you touch the ground, you have to start all over again.

Warning *Before attempting a full circuit, it is essential to perfect the techniques—leaping, balancing, hanging, and so on. Also, plan your route in advance, so you don't end up stranded on the balcony wall with no exit strategy.*

Some typical maneuvers

- ➲ Leaping from an upturned wastebasket to the armchair
- ➲ Tightrope-walking along the radiator
- ➲ Swinging on the door frame out onto the balcony furniture
- ➲ Swinging on the bathroom door 180° from bedside table to desk
- ➲ The toilet-bidet-sink triple jump
- ➲ Traversing the windowsill, using the curtain rail for handholds
- ➲ Somersaulting across the bed from one bedside table to the other

3. Leap to bedside table (watch the light).

4. Using bed as trampoline, bounce to top of wardrobe (if ceiling is low, you will have to crouch).

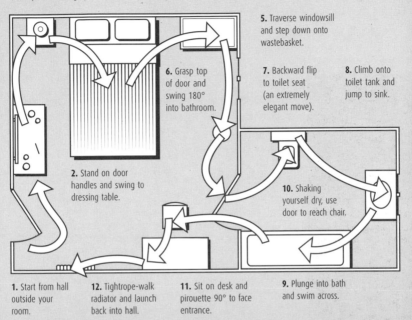

5. Traverse windowsill and step down onto wastebasket.

6. Grasp top of door and swing 180° into bathroom.

7. Backward flip to toilet seat (an extremely elegant move).

8. Climb onto toilet tank and jump to sink.

2. Stand on door handles and swing to dressing table.

10. Shaking yourself dry, use door to reach chair.

1. Start from hall outside your room.

12. Tightrope-walk radiator and launch back into hall.

11. Sit on desk and pirouette 90° to face entrance.

9. Plunge into bath and swim across.

Tip one | *You can construct a practice route for novices by arranging furniture around the edge of the room first.*

Tip two | *If you have to make a spectacular leap, it's best done to or from the bed, which of course forms a natural trampoline.*

Tip three | *Before you try hanging from anything, make sure it will hold your weight.*

In-Line Tray Skating

YOU WILL NEED

- SUGAR GLUE
  (see page 17)
- SLIPPERS
- SMALL TRAYS
- ASHTRAY
- UMBRELLA OR BROOM

Many hotels have a gym and a pool, but precious few have a skating rink. Or do they? Well, yes, if you include the hotel hobbyist's homemade one. Clear all the furniture to one corner of the room, and you've got an expanse of floor crying out to be glided upon. Skates are no problem either: a couple of those little trays you didn't return to room service attached to a pair of slippers—the ones you get on posh airlines are ideal. There's nothing stopping you. Except perhaps that end wall.

Tip| *If your room is not carpeted, or you want to utilize the bathroom, you must modify your skates—tie towels onto the bottom of the trays. This has the added bonus of cleaning up any spills from your messier hobbies.*

1| Mix a large portion of sugar glue and use it to stick your slippers firmly to a pair of little trays.

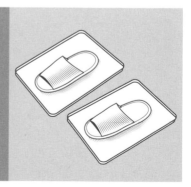

ON THIN ICE

Slip your feet into the slippers, and off you go. Push with one foot, glide with the other. Until you get the hang of it, practice skating in a straight line. When you feel more confident, try some of the trickier moves.

ICE HOCKEY

Once you've perfected the techniques, why not try a little hockey practice? Use the ashtray as a puck, and an umbrella for the stick (or borrow a broom from the hotel cleaner).

SOME FLASHY STUFF

GLIDING Glide along on one foot, arms outstretched, the other leg raised behind you (not as easy as it looks).

SKATING BACKWARD Build up a little momentum going forward first, then do the turn. You must remember to look over your shoulder to avoid obstacles.

PIROUETTE Spin on one foot while pushing with the other (flinging your arms around also helps).

BALLETIC LEAPS Just about feasible for the amateur tray skater, but toe-loops, lutzes, salchows, and the like are best left to the pros.

5

ENTERTAIN YOURSELF

Go back a hundred years or more, before the days of TV, radio, or computer games, and you'll be surprised to find that few people got bored. Sure, working hours were long, and there were few labor-saving devices, but people knew how to use their leisure time. Families would eat around the table together, then play games or sing around the piano, or try to improve themselves by reading an inspirational book or taking up some educational hobby or craft. Necessity was the mother of invention—if they couldn't get to the theater, they made one, raiding the wardrobes for dress-up clothes and then writing and acting out their own plays.

It's time you took a page out of your grandparents' book and rediscovered the joy of entertaining yourself. You'll find how enriching it can be to settle down with a good book or to learn basic science from simple experiments. Better still, give your inner Spielberg free rein and make yourself the writer, director, and star of your own shows. It's got to be better than vegging out in front of game shows, soaps, and repeats of 1970s sitcoms.

Bible NASDAQ

Trying to crack hidden codes has been in vogue recently, especially Bible-related cryptics. I suppose it all started with Kurt Vonnegut's *Sirens of Titan*, where the hero chooses which stock company to invest in by taking the first letters of words in the Good Book and looking for a quoted company starting with those letters. Maybe he was on to something—and maybe you can crack the code buried in your Gideon's Bible that will turn it into the ultimate investment guide and lead you to untold wealth. But remember, prices can go down as well as up: the Lord giveth, and the Lord taketh away.

Warning| *Linking the Good Book with the forces of Mammon may offend some people's religious sensibilities. Actually, it doesn't much matter what book you use, so long as you feel it has some authority— Shakespeare, Dickens, Poe . . . maybe even Stephen King has cleverly encoded the secrets of the stock exchange.*

Now the snake was the cunning animal that the God had made. The snake the woman, "Did God rea you not to eat fruit fror tree in the garden?" "We may eat the fruit (tree in the garden,"the wo

1| Open your Gideon's Bible to a random page. Close your eyes and stab at the page with a pin or your finger. This is your starting point.

Now the snake was the cunning animal that the (God) (had) (m)ade. The snake the woman, "Did God rea you not to eat fruit fror tree in the garden?"

"We may eat the fruit c tree in the garden,"the wo

2| Take the first letter of each word in order, and write it down. When you've got a meaningful series of letters, consult the financial pages of your newspaper.

3| See if you can find a company whose name corresponds in some mysterious way with the letters that you selected . . . then call your broker.

THE FIBONACCI SERIES

This is formed by starting with 0 and 1 and then adding the latest two numbers to get the next one. This sequence is found in natural phenomena, so perhaps it contains some mystical key to wealth.

0 1 1 2 3 5 8 13 21 34 55 89 144

PRIME NUMBERS

Prime numbers are those that can not be divided by any number other than themselves or one. Again, they can provide a sequence of letters in your source book, be it a Bible or a novel.

2 3 5 7 11 13 17 19 23 29 31 37 41 43 47 53 59 61 67 71 73 79 83 89 97 101 103 107 109 113 127 131 137 139 149 151 157 163 167 173 179 181 191 193 197 199 211 223 227 229 233 239 241 251 257 263 . . .

Tip| *You can take every prime-numbered (or Fibonacci-sequenced, or whatever) word from a page at random and see if it gives you any clues.*

Tea Bag Puppetry

YOU WILL NEED

- TEA BAGS
- DENTAL FLOSS
- TOOTHPICKS
- MAGAZINES
- MANILA FOLDERS
- PAPER NAPKINS

The roar of the greasepaint, the smell of the crowd . . . if you've ever been bitten by the acting bug, you'll really miss the stage while you're away. But you've got all the equipment you need to set up your own theater company and produce hit shows. Tea bags become a talented cast, and superfluous manila folders can be transformed into a booth or even a full proscenium arch. And your role in all of this? Founder, scriptwriter, stage crew, ultimate actor-manager—and audience and critic too.

Some suggestions to get you going . . .

Don't be too conservative in writing the script for your puppet show. Traditionalists might like to stick to Punch and Judy or a well-known fairy tale, but there's scope for all sorts of genres— Greek tragedy, Shakespearean comedy, farce, whodunit, or even Broadway musical. For a bit of modernist realism, you could role-play tomorrow's meeting.

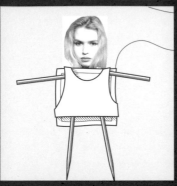

PUPPETS

Use tea bags on string as marionettes (if they are the type with no string, use dental floss). Give them arms and legs made from toothpicks, and cut out faces from magazines to create different characters. Make costumes from the little envelopes the tea bags come in. Or, use the envelopes as finger puppets for some of the minor roles.

THEATER

Unfold a manila folder and assemble either as a Punch and Judy–style booth or a traditional stage with paper-napkin curtains.

SCRIPT

Get in touch with your inner Shakespeare/Miller/Sondheim and put pen to paper, or discuss a plot for improvisation with your cast.

CRITICS

Don't worry about them. Write your own rave reviews.

PERFORMANCE

Stifle the first-night stage fright and get on with the show.

Synchronized Swishing

YOU WILL NEED

- REMOTE-CONTROL FOR TV, VIDEO, STEREO, DRAPES, BLINDS, LIGHTS, ETC.

- PAPER AND PEN

Clever marketing types have transformed some of the dullest monuments and natural landmarks into major tourist attractions by effective use of sound and lights. Perhaps you could do the same for your hotel room, turning it into a spectacular venue for son et lumière with you in charge via the remote controls to your gadgets. Picture it now . . . as the sun sets slowly over your balcony, the drapes pull back and a spotlight falls onto (cue dramatic music) the ancient wastebasket—who knows what secrets it contains?

1| Collect all the remotes for your lights, drapes, blinds, TV, video, etc. Choose a spot for your control desk. You may have to put this near the main light switch.

Tip| *Some older hotels have few, if any, remote-controlled facilities. Don't let this put you off; it just means a bit more preparation. Get all the switches, cords, and other controls as handy as possible. You may have to do a bit of running around, so make sure your script gives you time to get from one to the next.*

Welcome to Room 101. Many travelers before us have come through this ancient portal, and been astonished by the view across the vast expanse of double bed. But how many have explored the mysteries of the bedside table?

What secrets are hidden in its unassuming drawer? Who has had the courage to explore the depths of the cavernous wardrobe? So let us make the journey around this room, discovering its many delights—and maybe some surprises . . .

2| Devise a script with a commentary highlighting the main features of your room (balcony, bathroom, wardrobe, etc.), and position any movable lights.

3| Mark the script with lighting and music cues (it's a good idea to highlight these in different colors and label your remotes accordingly).

4| If you don't have suitable CDs, or even a CD player, take a chance on what's on the TV or radio at the time of the show. Choose your station carefully.

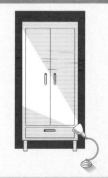

5| Wait for the sun to go down, turn down the lights, and do the show. Don't forget to use dimmers and volume controls as well as simple on and off.

Sleeping-Mask Superhero

By day, you are a mild-mannered sales rep or conference delegate, but who could have guessed that by night you haunt the upper floors of the hotel, rooting out the bad guys? As soon as danger threatens the planet, you dive into your closet and emerge as the masked savior of the universe! All you have to do to make this dream come true is make yourself a really cool costume, and the things you need are easily found in your room. Is it a bird? Is it a plane? No . . . it's (insert your choice of superhero name here)!

YOU WILL NEED

- SLEEPING MASK
- BEDCLOTHES, TOWELS

Warning| *This is a fantasy game. You are not really transformed into a being with superhuman powers just by donning a cape and mask. So don't overdo things—clambering up the outside of the hotel and flying from the balcony are out of the question. And if you do stumble across an arch-villain, try dialing 911.*

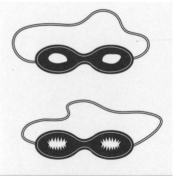

The mask| Cut out eyeholes from sleeping mask. Female superheroines might like eyelashes too.

THE CAPE

Depending on your size and stature, use a towel or bedclothes as a cape.

THE TOP

A tight T-shirt is a must. Boys can make a nifty logo from a paper napkin, girls can wear a bra or bikini top over the shirt.

THE BOTTOM

Underpants (or bikini bottom) should be worn outside pants or (better) panty hose.

THE ACCESSORIES

Gloves and boots are really cool if you have them, and a shower cap makes a good hood.

THE SUPERHERO

At the first sign of danger, leap into your closet or shower stall and change into your super outfit. Leap out, shouting a magic slogan of your choice ("Haile Selassi!" or "Hieronymous!" for instance). Hunt down evildoers and destroy them using your chosen superpowers (the strength of an elephant, the night vision of a cat, the smell of a dog . . . no, maybe not).

Shown here| *Gogetem Girl stalks the hotel hallways in a classic bra-over-T-shirt-and-panty-hose outfit with lovely bedspread cape, while Motel Man roots out evildoers in his shower cap, rubber gloves, briefs, and bath towel.*

Free Static

As part of the Hotel Science 101 course, you can learn how to generate static electricity from the friction of two objects composed of different materials—transferring electrons from one to the other and creating an excess of positive charge in one and negative in the other—and observe the effects of electrostatic adhesion, electrical discharge, and similar phenomena. In layman's terms, that's rubbing stuff together and seeing if it picks things up, makes sparks, or does anything useful.

Warning| *It goes without saying that you don't mess with electricity except in controlled conditions. Don't attempt any of these experiments near flammable substances or if you suffer from a cardiovascular disorder. The results could be shocking.*

YOU WILL NEED

- NYLON COMB
- PLASTIC PEN
- NYLON CLOTHES
- NYLON SHEETS
- LEATHER-SOLED SHOES

1| A simple instance of triboelectricity can be seen by combing dry hair with a nylon comb. Electrostatic adhesion can be observed in the attraction the loose hair has for the comb, and electrical discharges heard as a quiet crackle.

2| Similar phenomena can be observed by vigorously rubbing a plastic pen with a wool cloth. The pen develops the tendency to attract small, light objects such as pieces of paper and dust.

3| For more dramatic shows, quickly remove a nylon shirt or blouse in a darkened room, or rub a cotton-clothed or naked body against nylon sheets and swiftly pull back the bedclothes—the clinging effect of the clothes is due to static electricity.

4| Add to your superhero repertoire (*see page 88*) by shuffling over wool carpet while wearing leather-soled shoes. Literally zap visiting colleagues or room service staff with a touch of your electrostatically charged finger.

Bathrobe Couture

That shapeless bathrobe hanging in the bathroom may not seem the most stylish garment you've ever seen, but in the right hands it has the potential to take even Paris by storm. A few minor alterations, inspired by your favorite couturier, and it's ready to show. Use your bathroom as a changing room and make a catwalk from there through your room, perhaps setting out a few chairs for the press and celebs. Prepare a few different styles, practice your sashaying, and then wow the fashion world with your latest creations.

Tip| *Why restrict yourself to the bathroom when you create your wardrobe? There's a wealth of items in your room—drapes, lamp shades, bedclothes, and cushion covers can all form your next collection.*

YOU WILL NEED

- BATHROBE
- LAUNDRY BAG
- SLIPPERS
- TOWEL
- DIGITAL CAMERA

1| First select your bathrobe. Then adapt it to your chosen style.

FEMALE EVENING WEAR
Off the shoulders; use sleeves to hold up.

2| MALE SMART With tie made from bathrobe cord.

VARIATION: UNISEX CASUAL Undone, hands in pockets.

3| MACHO STREETWISE With hood, either robe pulled up over head or towel hood.

4| UNISEX AVANT-GARDE Deconstructed (put legs through arms of bathrobe and wrap it round you, tie in place with belt—think Jean-Paul Gaultier).

Accessories|
· Laundry bag: with or without dental-floss strap.
· Slippers: decorate with paper clips for evening wear.
· Hat: Make from towel (various ways of folding), or attach a brim to the shower cap.

Tip| Fashion need not be transient. A digital camera is all you require to attend your hotel catwalk as your very own fashion paparazzo.

Shadow Animals

This game's so old, they were doing it on cave walls in the Stone Age. It just needs a light source and a wall to project onto. Close the curtains, switch on the desk lamp, and point it at a clear space on the wall, then make shapes with your hands. With practice, you'll soon be able to make recognizable animal shadows and even make them move realistically. Add your own sound track ("Bird on a Wire," "Tiger Rag," etc.), and you have the makings of a great evening's entertainment.

Tip| *Once you have your hands around these, you can experiment with some animals of your own— a convincing snake, elephant, or bear, for instance (the armadillo may be a little ambitious).*

YOU WILL NEED

- DESK LAMP
- WALL

1| THE RABBIT Start simple. Possible sound tracks include:
- " I'm Gonna Wash That Man Right Outta My Hare"
- " Bunny Makes the World Go Round"

2| THE DOVE Moving on to two hands now. Possible sound tracks:
- "Dove Is in the Air"
- "What Is This Thing Called Dove?"

3| THE WOLF Starting to get tricky. Practice until you can make its mouth open and close. Possible sound tracks:
- "Howling Wolf Blues"
- "Bad Moon Rising"
- Anything by Mozart

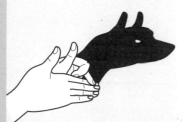

4| THE SWAN Moving on to advanced work. Possible sound tracks:
- "Just Swan of Those Things"
- "Swannee River"
- "Swanderful, Smarvellous" (Perhaps this could be your "cygneture" tune?)

6

GAMES & PASTIMES

There's a whole slew of computer games available for you to while away your time on your laptop, but anybody who has spent an evening playing these will tell you just how mind-numbingly dull and ultimately pointless they are. Why bother, when there are so many other games that have stood the test of time and offer intellectual stimulation, creative challenge, or a chance to practice your skills? With just a little preparation, you can have a whole compendium of games in your room and the satisfaction of having made them all yourself.

Some, like golf and basketball, are games you already play at home or have always wanted to try; others are those you remember from when you were a kid, such as checkers, solitaire, and snap, or fantasy games like dressing up, making yourself a hideaway, or finding an imaginary friend. Now, don't they sound better than virtual solitaire, electronic arcade games, and violent video games? So, pack up the laptop, forget the dubious temptation of digital trickery, and get on with the real thing—it's playtime!

Olive Golf

YOU WILL NEED

- CREAMERS AND SUGAR FROM THE COFFEE TRAY
- TOWEL
- ASHTRAY
- OLIVES
- TEASPOON
- COFFEE MIXER
- TOOTHBRUSH
- NAIL FILE

Fed up with lugging your clubs around on the off chance you might get a round in during your sales trip? Olive golf guarantees a game whenever you want, without the hassle or expense. And because you design your own course, you can play to your strengths or practice your weaker strokes. Another attraction is the eccentric aerodynamic characteristics of the olive pit. Any fool can play with a round ball, but it takes a real pro to cope with a knobbly oval—putting presents a particular challenge, especially on carpet.

Tip| *Good course design is vitally important to a satisfactory round of olive golf. The right mix of straightforward and tricky holes, scenic fairways, and interesting hazards makes all the difference. A nice touch is to place your final green just next to the minibar, so you can have a celebratory shot at the nineteenth hole.*

1| Roughly map out a course around your hotel room floor. It's probably a bit ambitious to go for the full eighteen holes, so aim for nine. Try to get as much variety as possible—different lengths, doglegs, etc.

2| Use the little creamers from your coffee set as holes, then add a few hazards. Use sugar as a sand trap, a towel for the rough, and fill an ashtray to create a water hazard.

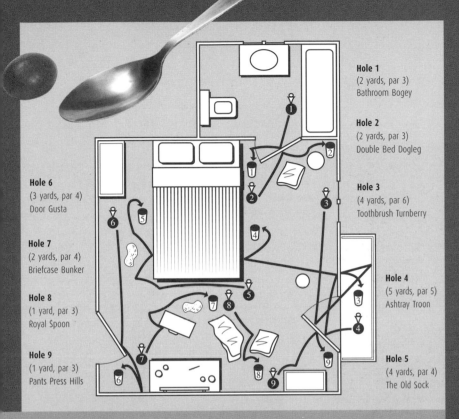

Hole 1
(2 yards, par 3)
Bathroom Bogey

Hole 2
(2 yards, par 3)
Double Bed Dogleg

Hole 3
(4 yards, par 6)
Toothbrush Turnberry

Hole 4
(5 yards, par 5)
Ashtray Troon

Hole 5
(4 yards, par 4)
The Old Sock

Hole 6
(3 yards, par 4)
Door Gusta

Hole 7
(2 yards, par 4)
Briefcase Bunker

Hole 8
(1 yard, par 3)
Royal Spoon

Hole 9
(1 yard, par 3)
Pants Press Hills

3| Work out a par for each hole, and a name. Maybe give yourself a handicap (as if you need any more handicaps).

4| Place an olive pit at the beginning of the course, and tee off. Use teaspoons, coffee mixers, toothbrushes, and nail files as clubs (you'll soon discover which make good drivers, wedges, or putters).

5| Make your way around the course, keeping a scorecard. End with a snifter or two at the clubhouse, recounting the tale of the near hole-in-one at the long sixth, or the incident of the pigeon on the balcony at the third green.

Olive Pit Checkers

A classic game of cunning and ruthlessness, adapted so you can play away matches without having to cart the board around with you on business trips. To make the most of this, it's best to invite a colleague—or better still, a business rival—around for a few martinis in your room. Once you've got the drinks poured, suggest an intellectual tussle over the checkerboard. Drink the cocktails, save the olive pits, and then decide who plays what—black or green? Pit your wits with the pits, and may the best hobbyist win.

YOU WILL NEED

· OLIVES (GREEN AND BLACK, 12 OF EACH) OR OTHER COCKTAIL SNACKS

· NAPKIN CHESSBOARD
(see page 44)

Tip| *If you manage to get to your opponent's side of the board with one of your pits and want to make it into a king, you're going to have problems: you just can't stack olive pits. One solution is to replace it with, for instance, a peach pit or bottle top.*

1| Drink martinis and save the olive pits.

2| You will need green and black olives for different-colored pits, or you could try playing olive pits against peanuts, or cashews against macadamias.

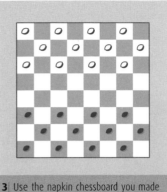

3| Use the napkin chessboard you made for the minibar chess (*see page 44*), and set out your pieces.

Shown here| *Let battle commence. If for some unaccountable reason you can't persuade a colleague to join you, you can either play yourself or set up a long-distance game with a friend via camera phones.*

103

Wet Tea Bag Dunk

There can't be anyone who hasn't at some time or another tossed their squeezed tea bag across the room and into the wastebasket, cheering a successful throw or bemoaning a failure. For a moment, you're a basketball star, and all eyes are on you as you line up for this crucial shot. Wet tea bag dunk is a refinement of this simple activity, which gives you the chance to practice your slam dunks from the comfort of your hotel bed and constructively use the time you would have spent just sitting and sipping your tea.

1| Use a paper cup for a basket, and choose a suitable spot some distance from the bed. Secure by wedging with heavy objects such as a hairbrush.

Tip| *The secret of success in this game lies very much in getting the optimum wetness of the tea bag. Too wet, and the bag has no bounce—it just splats against the back wall with predictably messy consequences; too dry, and it's difficult to throw with any accuracy.*

2| The cup could be placed against a vertical surface such as a wall, mirror, or wardrobe door. Ideally, use sugar glue to stick it firmly to its backboard.

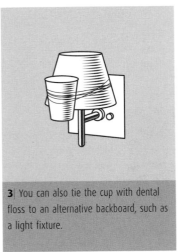

3| You can also tie the cup with dental floss to an alternative backboard, such as a light fixture.

Shown here| *Save up your used tea bags. If they're the type with string, remove this, being careful not to tear or burst the bag. Throw tea bags one by one, noting your progress. Challenge yourself by placing the cup in more difficult positions, or trying trick shots (throwing over your shoulder with your back to the cup, from between your legs, blindfolded, or while asleep).*

Ice Cube Solitaire

YOU WILL NEED

• TRAY

• TOOTHPASTE

• ICE CUBES

There are a few games specifically designed for just one player, and solitaire has to be the best known. You're not so much playing yourself as pitting your wits against the board itself—and this version introduces the element of playing against the clock too. The object is to remove pieces until there is only one remaining, at the center of the board; the time limit is that you have to do it before it all melts. If you succeed, reward yourself with a scotch on the rocks and remember Julius Caesar: I came, I thaw, I conquered.

Warning| *Speed is the name of the game, since your pieces are fast disappearing, but too much haste can be counterproductive. Ice cubes are slippery little devils. Pick them up carefully or they will fly off in all directions.*

1| Mark out the board on a tray using toothpaste. Make sure each square is big enough to hold an ice cube, and the squeeze of toothpaste is generous enough to keep the cubes from slipping around.

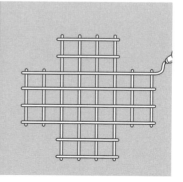

2 Set up the game, using twenty-four ice cubes and leaving a gap in the center of the board. Play by jumping one cube over another, into a gap.

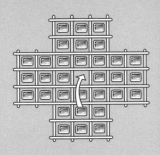

3 Every time you jump a cube, remove the jumped one and put it in the drink you poured yourself earlier. This will need refreshing throughout the game, which will consequently become more enjoyable.

4 To achieve victory, you should end up with only one cube, right in the middle of the board. And you should still be coherent enough to speak.

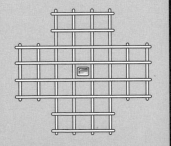

Cell Phone Snap

This has more in common with those "spot the difference" puzzles in cheap newspapers than the card game Snap, but the principle is the same. First of all, you need to call a colleague in another room or hotel and challenge him or her to a game. You then take turns photographing stuff in your rooms, using the camera on your cell phone, trying to copy the image you've just received. You'll be amazed how much fun this is—especially the arguments over what constitutes an acceptably true likeness.

YOU WILL NEED

- CAMERA PHONE
- COLLEAGUE OR FRIEND IN ANOTHER HOTEL ROOM

Tip| *Keep it simple to start off with, using things that you know are found easily in any hotel room. This will lull your opponent into a false sense of security. But look around for anything unusual in your room (a dead plant, for example). Keep this up your sleeve until you're ready to deliver the coup de grâce.*

1| Take a picture of an area of your room (dressing table, sink, etc.) and send it to your opponent.

2 Your opponent tries to match your picture precisely in his or her room, takes a picture, and sends it back to you.

3 If this matches, your opponent then takes a turn to add to—or subtly change—the arrangement and sends it for you to match . . . and so on.

4 Continue until one of you fails to give a satisfactory match (getting the layout wrong, missing an item, using an unacceptable substitute).

Play on *Figure out a system of scoring between yourselves, and play a set of games. Points should be awarded for creativity, exceptionally unsuitable items used to mimic an arrangement, surprise "joker" items, and so on. Let that imagination run wild.*

Room Service Memory Game

This is an update of that standby game at kids' parties. You show the kids a tray full of stuff, take it away, and they have to remember what was on the tray. If it's too easy, try again with more stuff on the tray. The winner is the kid who remembers most. That's it, basically. Deceptively simple in concept, and maddeningly difficult to play, it could keep you occupied for hours. Unless, of course, you cheat.

YOU WILL NEED

· TRAY

· RANDOM ITEMS

· TOWEL

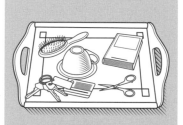

1| On your tray, lay out a selection of small items from among your possessions, the hotel room, or what you can get from room service.

Tip| *For a more challenging game, try adding more items to the tray, increasing the count to 100, or having a few drinks before making your list. Even harder—prepare the tray in the morning, and when you come back in the evening, try to remember where you left your keys.*

2 Cover tray with a towel and slowly count to thirty.

1. keys
2. book
3. cuddly toy
4. ermm...

3 Write down everything on the tray that you can remember.

Shown here Whip off the towel and check against your list. Award yourself points for correct answers and penalties for wrong or missed ones. As a variation on the original game, put in a complicated order to room service. While waiting for it, see how much of it you can remember. When it arrives, check against your list.

Blow-Dryer 007

Dum diddle-um dum, da da da, dum diddle-um dum, da da da . . . Stirred into action, not shaken by the evil mastermind, you suavely insinuate yourself into his hideout for the final showdown. You're licensed to kill, and with just your trusty blow-dryer, you mow down all his fiendish minions and catch him in his lair. It just remains for you to finish him off, rescue the girl, and return to M with the secret documents—and not a hair out of place. Okay, it's only a game, but what the heck? Lights, camera—action!

Some suggestions to get you going . . .

Put on your tux and bow tie. Pick up your blow-dryer and pose in front of a full-length mirror. Impressive, eh? It's safer to unplug the blow-dryer before attempting any of this. Leaping around the room attached to the outlet is not recommended, and it will restrict your movements unnecessarily. If you really want to have the dryer ready for action, see if you can get hold of a cordless one. You're set for a blow-dry Blofeld. (*See also warning on page 88.*)

(See also warning on page 88.)

YOU WILL NEED

- BLOW-DRYER
- TUXEDO
- LITTLE BLACK DRESS

BONDING

Select your favorite Bond before attempting a convincing impression. You have to know what your motivation is, darling. You could be Connery, Moore, Brosnan, whoever— or perhaps even Mish Moneypenny.

BOND MOMENT

Act out your favorite Bond moments: leap out of the wardrobe, blow-dryer blazing; fit the silencer (that weird nozzle thing) and snipe from behind the curtain; roll under the bed while firing a volley at the balcony; kick open the bathroom door and spray the guy in the shower.

HUDSON HAWK?

If you're not a Bond fan (surprisingly, not everyone is), choose another action hero—Gibson, Willis, Glover, or Schwarzenegger, say—and dress yourself accordingly.

BOND GIRL

Don't get left out just because you're a girl. There have been some pretty impressive females in the Bond films. Or you could do an Angelina Jolie or the *Charlie's Angels* thing

Balcony Scarecrow

The scarecrow is a perennial favorite in kids' stories and wins most people's hearts for simply being outstanding in his field. But we can't forget what this lovable scruff bag was designed to do—scare crows. If you're worried about security—or you've simply been alone too long—make yourself an urban scarecrow. Sit him on the balcony to deter cat burglars, in your bed to discourage light-fingered cleaning staff, or at your desk to provide a reassuring, friendly presence and someone to talk to when you can't sleep.

Tip| *It can get mighty lonely in hotel rooms, and your scarecrow makes a good (if quiet) companion, or a worthy opponent in some of the two-person games. Or, you could play CSI, using him as your ketchup-spattered murder victim—draw around the body on the floor, and mark the trajectory of the bullets with dental floss and thumbtacks.*

1| Wrap two pillows, end to end, in your bathrobe; one pillow should protrude slightly to form the head, the other held in place with the bathrobe belt.

2| Stuff the bottom end of the lower pillow into the top of a pair of pants, then stuff towels into the arms and legs to give them some bulk.

3| Make a convincing head shape by tying dental floss around the pillow to form a neck.

4| Put on a pair of eyeglasses, shades, or a sleeping mask, and paint on a face with lipstick, shoe polish, or a felt-tip pen.

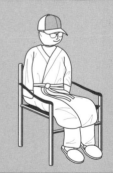

5| Slip on a pair of slippers and put your finished scarecrow on the chair on the balcony in the sun. Arrange his limbs in a convincing pose.

Make Your Own Yurt

Modern hotels may have all the latest in facilities and creature comforts, but let's face it, they're not exactly cozy, are they? If you find your room too big, too stark, or simply too much like a hotel, convert it into an authentic yurt—the traditional dwelling of the nomads of Mongolia. Yurts are light, warm, robust, and, well, sort of snug. Once you're ensconced in your personal yurt, you'll feel a million miles away from so-called civilization, and the noises from outside could so easily be a herd of grazing yaks . . .

YOU WILL NEED

- BEDCLOTHES
- DENTAL FLOSS
- A BROOM OR TWO (BORROWED FROM THE JANITOR'S CLOSET)

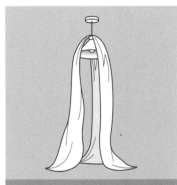

1| It's best to start from the middle of the room, attaching sheets, etc. to the central light fixture with dental floss.

Tip| *If you don't have enough fixtures, use brooms propped against the wall, wedged in place with the desk and chairs. Also be sure that your yurt has flaps that can be pulled to one side to allow access to the doors. Being trapped in a yurt when room service arrives can be highly frustrating—and a little embarrassing.*

2| Drape the sheets onto furniture around the walls to form the roof of your yurt. Secure with broom.

3| Use blankets and towels to make the walls by hanging them from the same fixtures.

Tip| *If you've developed a taste for the great indoor outdoors, you might like to try building a different sort of ethnic dwelling—a tepee, perhaps. Or, with the ice from the minibar, it's as easy as Eskimo pie to construct a miniature igloo. Since the results are far from permanent, this one is best quickly photographed for posterity.*

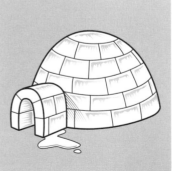

7

BATHROOM FUN

Remember when you were a kid, how your mom insisted that you take a bath? Even if you'd already had one that month? After some negotiation, you reluctantly conceded and trudged off to the bathroom. Hours later, you emerged, having had the time of your life playing with all that interesting stuff. You see, the bathroom is the best room in the house for having fun. There's just so much you can do in there, and you get the privacy you need to do it without inhibition or interruption. Of course, you could just lie back and relax in a hot tub, but that would be a waste—you'd miss out on all the good stuff.

Bathrooms have great acoustics for a start, and most of us can't resist the temptation to sing, or at least talk to ourselves. And there's a positive cornucopia of bottles, sprays, tubes, and utensils that has the same fascination as a well-stocked pharmacy. But the main attraction is, of course, the unlimited supply of water, offering no end to the possibilities for sports, games, and experiments. In short, the perfect playroom for the hotel hobbyist.

Toothbrush Karaoke

- TOOTHBRUSH

- VOICE

You're wasted in middle management, and you know it. Given the right break, you could have been up there with Sinatra and Garland. If only you could have found the right studio to develop your talents. Don't despair—there's a rehearsal room right next door where you can prepare a few numbers for the day you get discovered. Use your bathroom to hone your studio techniques. The acoustics are just about perfect for vocal performance—this is probably what bathrooms were designed for in the first place.

Tip| *If you lack the confidence to do a solo unaccompanied set, take your portable radio or CD player in to sing along to. And if your tastes are more Hendrix than Sinatra, use your toothbrush holder as a mic stand, leaving both hands free to hammer out a few guitar riffs on the loofah or back-scrubbing brush.*

1| Brush your teeth until you achieve a gleaming Hollywood smile. The perfect image is essential to success.

2| Rinse and dry your toothbrush. The microphone is the singer's most precious tool, and it needs to be kept pristine.

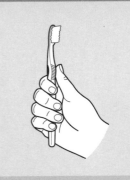

3| Hold your toothbrush up in front of your mouth. Posture is all.

4| Sing your favorite bathroom numbers. If you feel an overwhelming need to share your talent, use your cell phone for a live broadcast.

Advanced Work| Either stand in front of the mirror to appreciate the full visual effect, or go into the shower stall for enhanced acoustics. Use this recommended set list for your bathroom boogie:

· "Singin' in the Rain"
· "Easy Loofah"
· "Welcome, Toothy Hotel California"
· "Basin Street Blues"
· "There's No Business Like Shower Business"
· "Land of Soap and Glory"
· "God Shave the Queen"

Bath Tile Acrostics

The bathroom might not seem your first choice of place for doing word games, but when you think about it, it's actually perfect. Away from the phone, you can lie back in a relaxing hot tub and exercise the gray cells. You won't need paper, as the bathroom tiles provide a perfect writing surface, conveniently divided into squares, for lipstick writing; and you don't have to worry about finding an eraser—the walls can be wiped clean with your sponge or washcloth.

Warning| *Word games can be addictive. This is fine when you're sitting in an armchair, but in the bath can pose hazards. Beware of wrinkly skin and the risk of hypothermia as the bathwater cools.*

YOU WILL NEED

- LIPSTICK
- WATERPROOF DICTIONARY *(optional)*

1| ACROSTICS Write a word or phrase on a vertical column of tiles. Now fill in the horizontal rows with meaningful or poetic lines starting with these letters. If possible, do this in rhyming couplets, or even a more complex rhyme scheme.

I		L	I	K	E		T	O	S
R	U	B	-	A	-	D	U	B
V	A	C	A	T	E		M	Y	T
I	N		T	H	E		B	U	B	B
N	O		M	O	R	E		H	U	R
G	O	O	D	B	Y	E		W	O	R

2 | WORD SQUARES

Mark out a square of tiles for your word square. Enter a word both horizontally and vertically starting from the top left-hand corner. Move to the second row and column and enter another word, and continue until the square is complete. It's best to start with a simple 3x3 square, until you get the hang of this, then try 4x4 and work up to more.

B	A	T	H
A	R	E	A
T	E	S	T
H	A	T	S

3 | WORD TRANSFORMATION

Write a word horizontally on adjacent tiles. Choose a totally different word of the same number of letters, and write this down on the edge of the bath. Changing one letter at a time, write successive words under your original word, until you get to your target word. See how few steps you can do this in.

L	E	A	D
R	E	A	D
R	O	A	D
G	O	A	D
G	O	L	D

Tip | *Once you have devised your own bath tile crossword, you might want to invite visitors to take a bath and fill in the answers to your clues. Who knows what fun you could have?*

4 | CROSSWORDS

Design your own original crossword on a square of tiles. Decide how big you want this to be (anything up to about 15x15 tiles), and which squares you want to blank out. Now enter words into the grid where they will fit.

W	O	R	D	S		A	S	S
E		O		O		L		H
T	E	A		A	R	E	N	A
		S		P				V
B	A	T	H		T	I	M	E
R				H		N		
U	N	C	L	E		F	U	N
S		A		R		E		E
H	I	T		B	U	R	S	T

125

Shower Cap Paragliding

YOU WILL NEED

- SHOWER CAP

- DENTAL FLOSS, OR THREAD FROM EMERGENCY SEWING KIT

- SOAP

- NAIL FILE

Like a condor soaring on the thermals high up in the Andes, the shower cap paraglider floats silently down from the heights, taking in the spectacular views and landing smoothly miles below. Not a sport you immediately associate with bathrooms, it's true, but you can capture the magic of paragliding and the exhilaration of sky-diving in the hall, without any of the dangers. Forget expensive equipment, exotic locations, and extra insurance—you've got everything you need in the safety of your hotel.

1| Tie four six-inch lengths of thread or dental floss at regular intervals around the rim of a shower cap.

Troubleshooting

Failure of parachute to open can be caused by:

➲ Insufficient object mass —increase payload.

➲ Excessive object mass— decrease payload.

➲ Chute straps tangled— er, untangle.

➲ Shower cap too tightly folded—loosen up.

➲ Insufficient drop duration —increase height of launch; try launching from balcony.

2| Select a small object, perhaps a bar of soap carved into a human shape (*see page 18*). It should have sufficient mass to exert pull on the parachute strings.

3| The object should not be so massive as to counteract the decelerating drag of the parachute. Tie it securely to the trailing ends of the threads.

4| Fold the shower cap loosely and wrap around the object.

5| Launch the bundle from a height. This is best achieved by dropping from a window or throwing in a trajectory that nearly coincides with the ceiling.

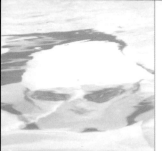

Bath Dunk

- BATHFUL OF WATER

- SPONGE

- SHOWER CAP

This is a bath-time variation on the Wet Tea Bag Dunk (*see page 104*). The goal of the game is to toss your sponge into a floating shower cap in order to gain points, wild applause, and fame—simple in concept but requiring patience, practice, and perseverance to master. There are many different shots you can try out, ranging from the simple drop shot through slam dunks and bank shots, to the over-the-shoulder lob and trick shots bounced off the sink or toilet. And no need to shower after a hard game!

Tip| *After unsuccessful shots, you will need to squeeze the sponge dry—if it's too wet, it won't bounce properly and may capsize or sink the shower cap.*

1| Open out a shower cap and float it upside down in your bath. Experiments show that bubble bath provides a good surface and keeps the shower cap from drifting. Bath salts are alleged to aid buoyancy, but this is not yet proven.

2| Take a sponge, small enough to fit easily into the shower cap, and squeeze it dry. Devise a points system: e.g., 1 for landing in shower cap, 2 for bouncing off a wall first, 3 for two walls, 4 for ricocheting around the rim of the toilet.

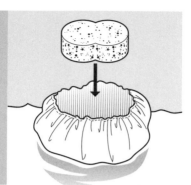

3| Throw the sponge, trying to land it in the shower cap. Depending on how athletic you're feeling, this can be done from a standing position. Experienced hobbyists generally prefer to remain horizontal in the bath.

4| See how many points you can score before the bathwater gets cold. There are, of course, penalty points for sinking the shower cap or getting your big toe trapped in one of the taps.

Fizz Boats

This is Module Two of the Hotel Science 101 course—examining the motive power of the expansion of effervescent tablets in water and finding a practical application by harnessing this, using the principle of jet propulsion, to power a lightweight conveyance. Careful study of effervescent tablets shows that they create energy when immersed in water; this experiment reveals how this can be contained and exploited to provide a source of thrust in a simple transportation context. Oh, and you get to race your little boats, too.

Tip| *For competitive racing, you'll need to make your boats distinguishable from one another. Use different colored paper, decorate with permanent markers, and make pennants from toothpicks and paper.*

YOU WILL NEED

· BATHFUL OF WATER

· PAPER

· EFFERVESCENT HANGOVER OR VITAMIN C TABLETS *(denture-cleaning tablets don't fizz so effectively)*

· PERMANENT MARKER

· TOOTHPICKS

1| Fill bath. As you wait for this, construct a paper boat (steps a–n), using letter- or similar-sized sheets (agendas, handouts for today's meetings, etc.). This is the classic origami boat, based on the paper hat everybody knows how to do.

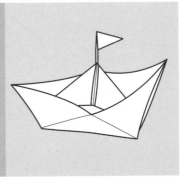

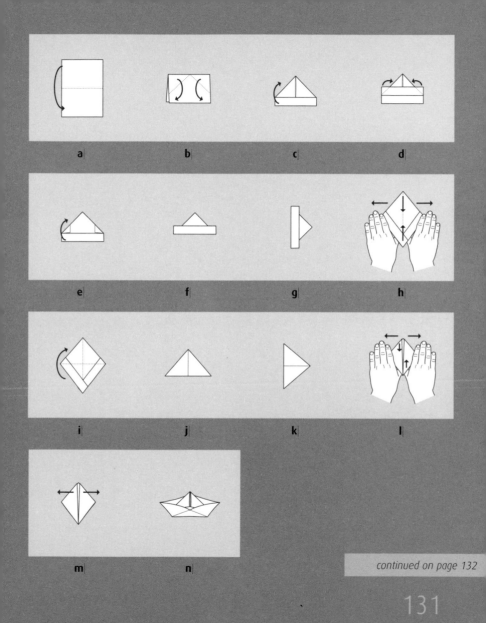

a| b| c| d|

e| f| g| h|

i| j| k| l|

m| n|

continued on page 132

131

Fizz Boats

2| Pull leading corner of boat forward to create a prominent bow, and flatten rear end to form a near-vertical stern.

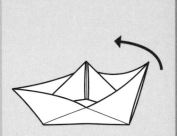

3| Insert effervescent tablet into the flap at the stern, ensuring that it is secure, below the anticipated waterline, and protruding slightly.

4| Gently float boat on bathwater, ensuring that the stern is lowered sufficiently into the water by the weight of the tablet to immerse it completely, but not so much as to risk totally submerging the boat.

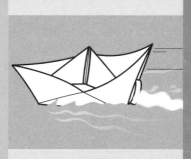

5| The force exerted by the expansion of the tablet due to effervescence should now act against the stern of the boat and propel it forward.

Troubleshooting

Failure to achieve propulsion may be due to:

➲ Inadequate immersion of tablet—make sure it is low down stern of boat and totally submerged.

➲ Total enclosure of tablet by structure of boat—ensure it protrudes adequately from its flap.

➲ Insufficient effervescence—check sell-by date of tablets.

➲ Excessive current of water in bath—allow Brownian motion to dissipate before trying again.

Tip *Having tested out your prototype, prepare a fleet of boats and stage a regatta.*

Soap on a Rope

- SOAP

- NAIL FILE

- BELT FROM YOUR
  BATHROBE

Perhaps the most underrated invention of the twentieth century, soap on a rope is a practical solution to the problem of storing slippery soap in the shower, combined with the aesthetic elegance of classic design. Unfortunately, many hotels have not yet gotten around to including this useful item in their array of complimentary goodies, and unless you remembered to bring your own, you're stuck with the familiar mushy mess in the waterlogged soap dish. Or are you? Not if you're a handy hotel hobbyist with a little time to spare!

Tip| *Handmade soap on a rope makes a neat gift to take home to your folks, or a handsome souvenir of your trip—especially if the soap has the name of your hotel on it. You might want to start a collection, saving soaps from around the world.*

1| Find the obligatory complimentary hotel soap in your bathroom, and unwrap it.

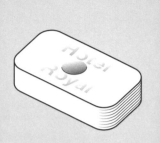

2| Make a hole in it using a nail file. You could also execute some Soap Scrimshaw at this point (*see page 18*).

3| Take the belt from your bathrobe and double it over, than make a knot to join the two ends together.

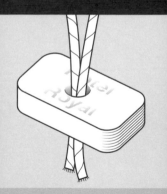

4| Thread the doubled-over end through the hole in the soap, ensuring the knot is big enough to stop the soap from falling off.

5| Tie another knot above the soap to hold it securely in place. Hang it up in your shower, or dangle it from your wrist.

Shaving Cream Sculpture

How many slabs of marble did Michelangelo get through before he created David . . . he had to practice on something first, didn't he? Shame he didn't have the benefit of a cheap and easy medium like shaving cream to work with. Still, it's now available to all us hotel sculptors and requires no specialized tools. Henry Moore–style abstract? No problem. Bust of a famous historical figure? Tricky, but possible. Statue of the Madonna and Child? Well, maybe it does have its limitations, but give it a try anyway.

Warning| *Sadly, the impermanence of the medium belies the maxim "ars longa, vita brevis." None of your masterpieces are going to survive the night, so preserve them for posterity with your cell phone camera.*

1| Squeeze out a generous amount of shaving cream onto a flat surface, such as the glass shelf above the sink.

2 Using a spoon and your fingers, form a lump of foam roughly into the shape you want.

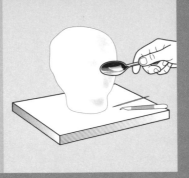

3 Using a toothpick, emery board, nail file, or spoon, carve in details to make a figure, face, animal, or whatever. Extra foam can be artfully added as necessary.

4 Try making cameo-type portraits on the bathroom mirror—but you'll have to work fast before it all slides down to the bottom. Ah, the tragic transience of modern art!

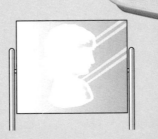

Crop Circles

- TOWELS
- WASHCLOTH
- BATH MAT
- HAIRBRUSH
  OR COMB

Some people still believe those crop circles that mysteriously appear overnight are created by human pranksters. It's far more likely that they are evidence of visitations by alien beings who just wanted to leave a calling card. And after your hotel stay, wouldn't you like to do the same? Leave something that really gets noticed, and has the staff talking about it for ages after you check out? Go on, then, make miniature crop circles in the nap of your towels, washcloth, and bathmat, or in the pile of the carpet.

Tip| *If you're staying a few days, you could combine this with the Hotel Farm project (see page 48) by scattering mustard and lettuce seeds onto wet towels and flattening the resulting crop into patterns. What do you mean, you haven't brought any seeds? I thought nobody traveled without them these days.*

1| HOW TO MAKE THEM Brush and comb against the grain, pressing flat—a traveling iron would be very useful if you have one.

2| SIMPLE CIRCLE Simple minimalist aliens have landed on the carpet.

3| DOUBLE SPIRAL Don't try this one after too many visits to the minibar.

4| YIN/YANG SYMBOL Balanced, Zen aliens make their harmonious mark.

5| COMPLICATED FRACTAL With this one, hotel staff will not merely remember your visit, but also be convinced you were an alien.

Wet Sliding

YOU WILL NEED

• SHOWER CURTAIN

• WATER

A combination of speed skating and the waterslides found at swimming pools, wet sliding is a sport requiring absolute physical fitness and nerves of steel. In a nutshell, it's not for wimps. Gliding across a treacherously slippery surface on bare feet at breakneck speed, struggling to keep your balance, and performing gravity-defying maneuvers is not everyone's idea of fun; but if you think you've got what it takes, you're in for the thrill of a lifetime. Or maybe a trip to the hospital. We, of course, do not recommend it.

Warning| *This is a much faster-moving sport than tray skating, and you have very limited time to do your turns and jumps before reaching the end of the rink. It's also more difficult to keep your balance, change direction, and slow down. To minimize possible injuries, you should surround your playing area with some soft furnishings.*

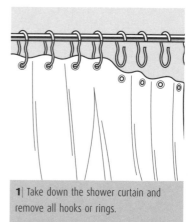

1| Take down the shower curtain and remove all hooks or rings.

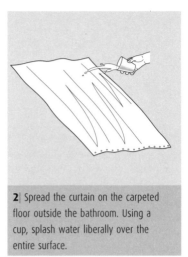

2| Spread the curtain on the carpeted floor outside the bathroom. Using a cup, splash water liberally over the entire surface.

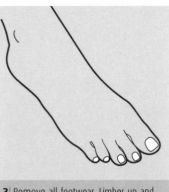

3| Remove all footwear. Limber up and prepare for death-defying antics.

Tip *Attempt some of the maneuvers outlined on page 76, In-line Tray Skating. The golden rule of Wet Sliding, espoused by all past and present champions, is that you should attempt to remain upright at all times.*

4| Take as much of a running start as you can from the hall, hurl yourself at the rink, and slide across.

Private Volcano

This is Module Three of the Hotel Science 101 course: examining the expansion of effervescent preparations in water, and relating this to the similar expansion of molten lava underground and its consequent upsurge through the earth's crust as volcanic eruption; an introduction to volcanology through the construction of a miniature volcano and simulation of eruption under controlled conditions. In other words, how to make a volcano and watch it erupt, cascading lather lava down the slopes of Krakatowel.

YOU WILL NEED

- WASHCLOTH OR HAND TOWEL

- CREAMER

- EFFERVESCENT HANGOVER OR VITAMIN C TABLETS

- SHAMPOO

- MOUTHWASH OR LIQUOR

Tip| *It will take some experimentation to find the optimum water/ shampoo/effervescent tablet ratio, and your first attempts might be a little disappointing. Once you've got the right proportions and a satisfactory overflow, try wrapping the creamer in plastic wrap and making a small hole in the top for a highly explosive eruption.*

1| Construct a small mountain (about the size of a molehill is good) with a concave indentation at the top, using a wet washcloth or hand towel.

2| Firmly embed a small container, for example an empty creamer from the coffee kit, in the base of the crater.

3| Drop an effervescent hangover or vitamin C tablet into the bottom of the creamer (if the tablet doesn't fit, break it into smaller pieces).

4| Add a teaspoon of shampoo and then enough water to cover the tablet and shampoo—add drops of mouthwash or liqueur for colored lava.

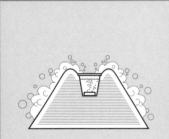

5| Watch it erupt. Notice how it mimics a real volcano: the pressure of expanding foam (lava) forces it up into the crater, then it flows down the mountainside.

Index